BEGINNING TO END

Potato to French Fry

by Elizabeth Neuenfeldt

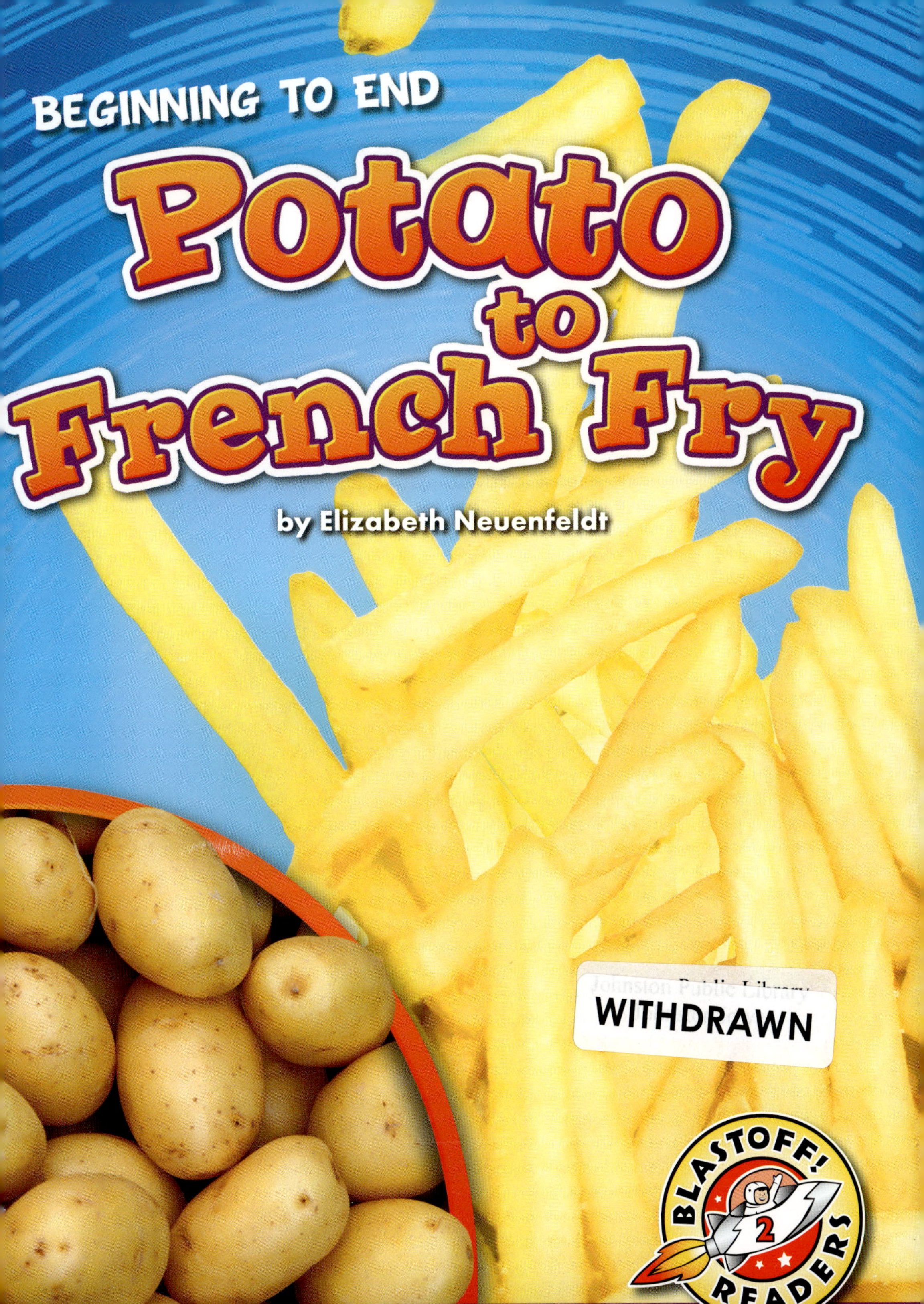
BLASTOFF! READERS
2

BELLWETHER MEDIA • MINNEAPOLIS, MN

Blastoff! Readers are carefully developed by literacy experts to build reading stamina and move students toward fluency by combining standards-based content with developmentally appropriate text.

Level 1 provides the most support through repetition of high-frequency words, light text, predictable sentence patterns, and strong visual support.

Level 2 offers early readers a bit more challenge through varied sentences, increased text load, and text-supportive special features.

Level 3 advances early-fluent readers toward fluency through increased text load, less reliance on photos, advancing concepts, longer sentences, and more complex special features.

★ **Blastoff! Universe**

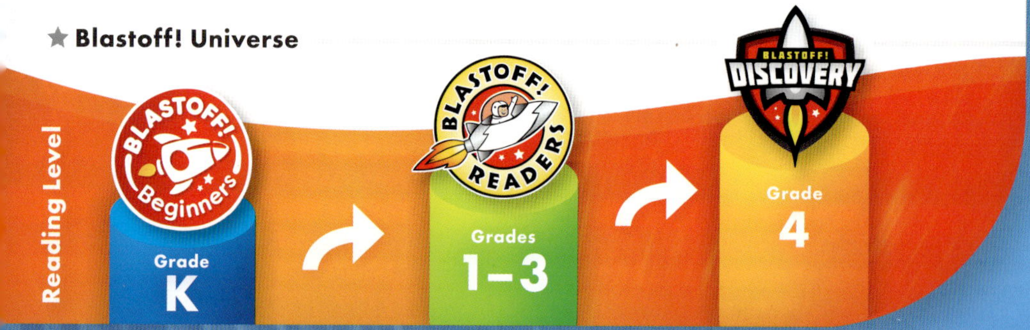

Reading Level

This edition first published in 2021 by Bellwether Media, Inc.

No part of this publication may be reproduced in whole or in part without written permission of the publisher. For information regarding permission, write to Bellwether Media, Inc., Attention: Permissions Department, 6012 Blue Circle Drive, Minnetonka, MN 55343.

Library of Congress Cataloging-in-Publication Data

Names: Neuenfeldt, Elizabeth, author.
Title: Potato to French fry / Elizabeth Neuenfeldt.
Description: Minneapolis, MN : Bellwether Media, Inc., 2021. | Series: Beginning to end | Includes bibliographical references and index. | Audience: Ages 5-8 | Audience: Grades K-1 | Summary: "Relevant images match informative text in this introduction to how potatoes become French fries. Intended for students in kindergarten through third grade"– Provided by publisher.
Identifiers: LCCN 2020039239 (print) | LCCN 2020039240 (ebook) | ISBN 9781644874240 (library binding) | ISBN 9781648342462 (paperback) | ISBN 9781648341014 (ebook)
Subjects: LCSH: French fries–Juvenile literature. | Potatoes–Juvenile literature. | Cooking (Potatoes)–Juvenile literature.
Classification: LCC TX803.P8 N39 2021 (print) | LCC TX803.P8 (ebook) | DDC 641.6/521–dc23
LC record available at https://lccn.loc.gov/2020039239
LC ebook record available at https://lccn.loc.gov/2020039240

Text copyright © 2021 by Bellwether Media, Inc. BLASTOFF! READERS and associated logos are trademarks and/or registered trademarks of Bellwether Media, Inc.

Editor: Rebecca Sabelko   Designer: Laura Sowers

Printed in the United States of America, North Mankato, MN.

Table of Contents

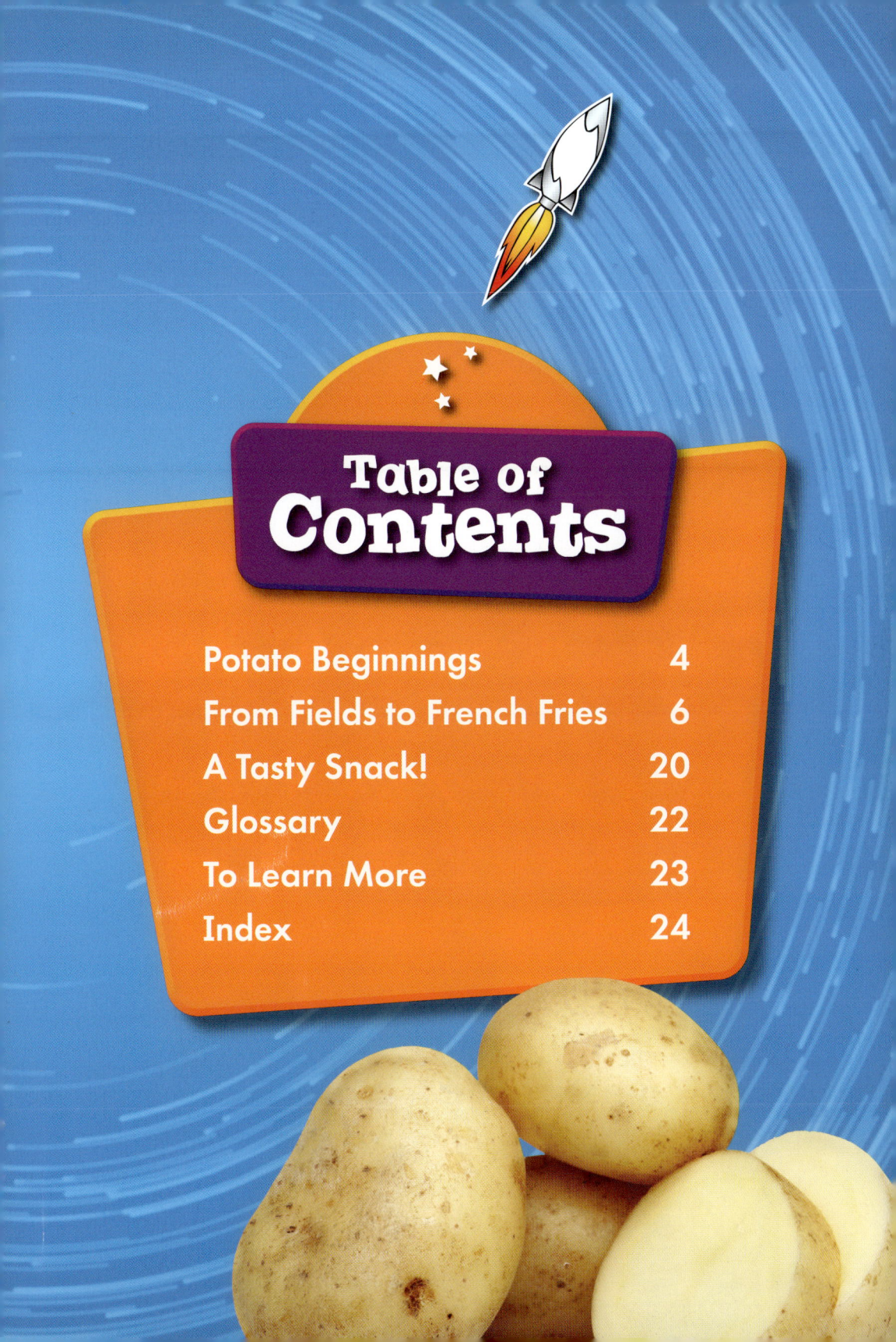

Potato Beginnings	4
From Fields to French Fries	6
A Tasty Snack!	20
Glossary	22
To Learn More	23
Index	24

Potato Beginnings

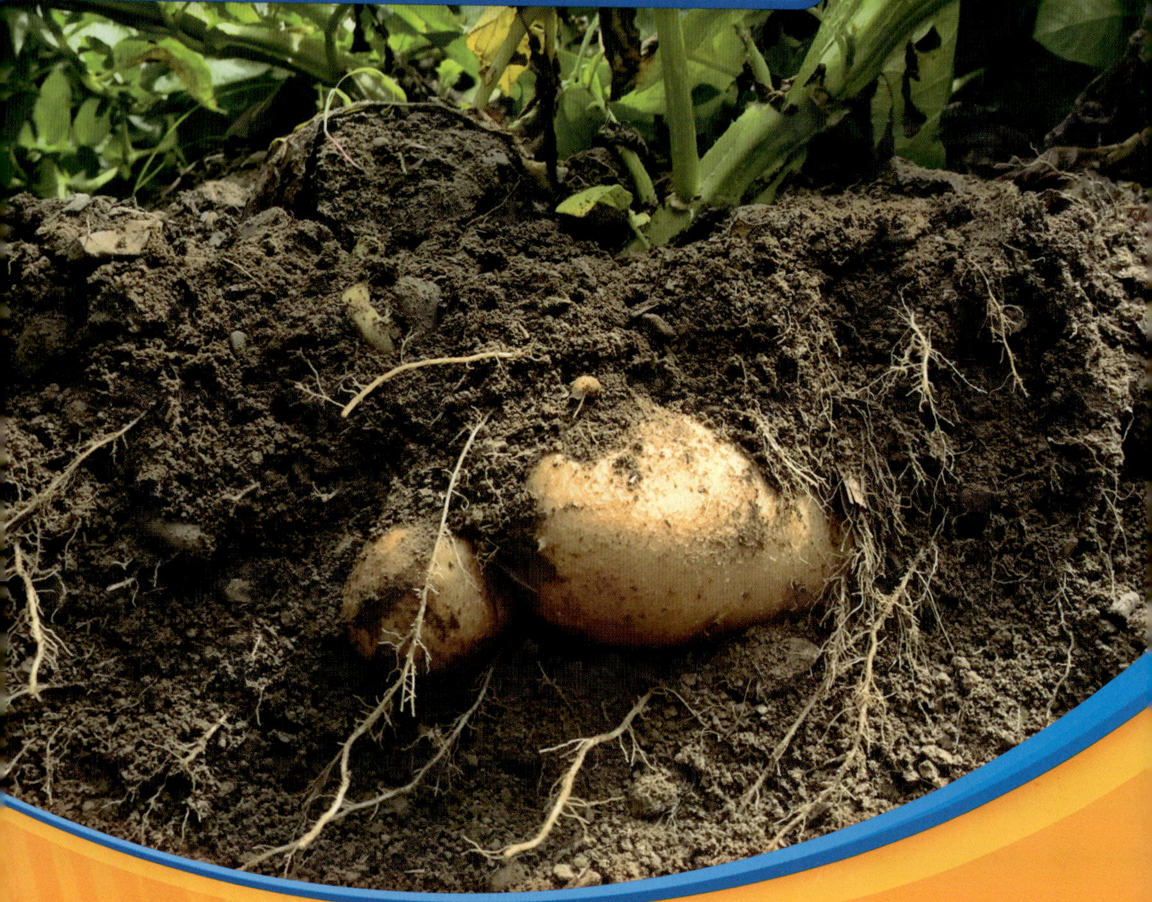

Did you know french fries come from potatoes?

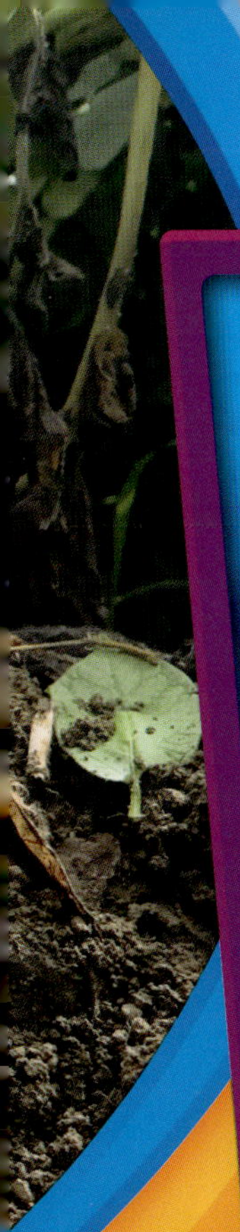

Where Do Potatoes Grow?

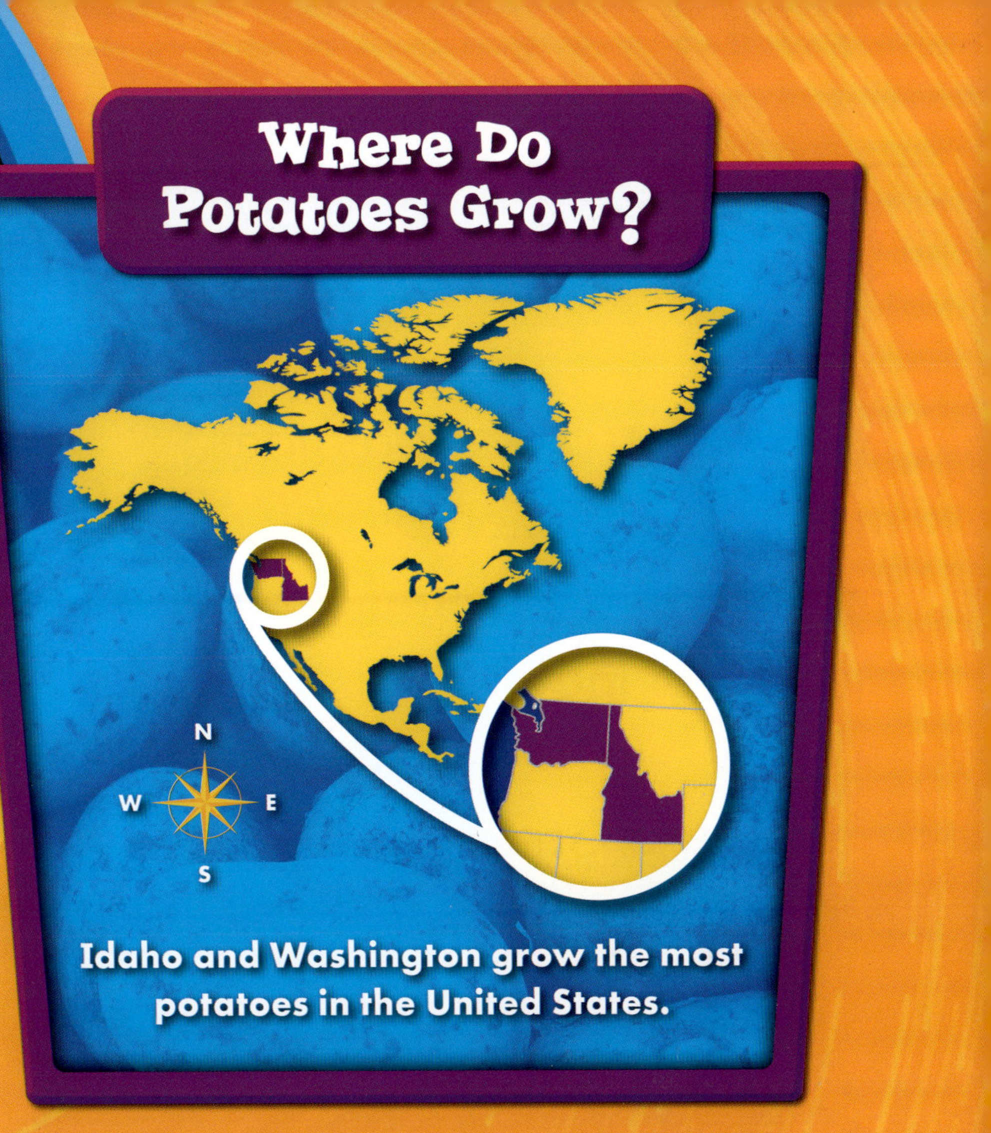
N
W
E
S

Idaho and Washington grow the most potatoes in the United States.

Potatoes grow on farms. These **root vegetables** grow underground!

From Fields to French Fries

Farmers **harvest** potatoes in spring, summer, or fall. Potato harvesters remove them from the ground.

Then trucks bring the potatoes to factories.

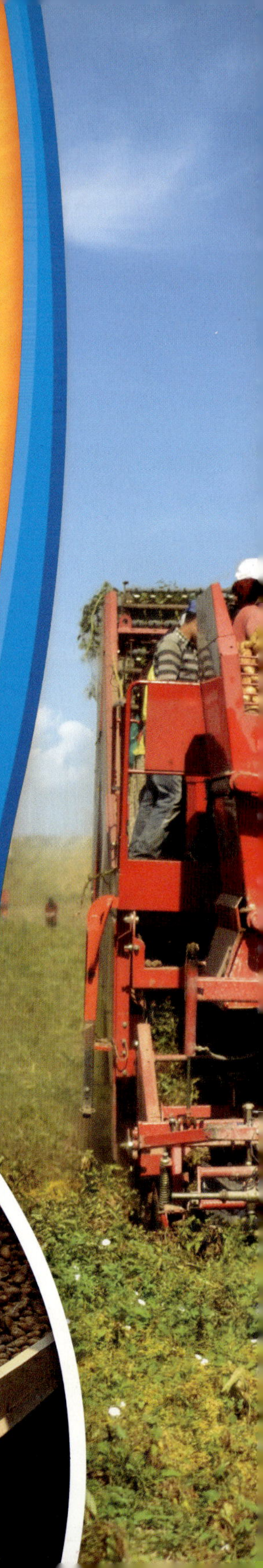

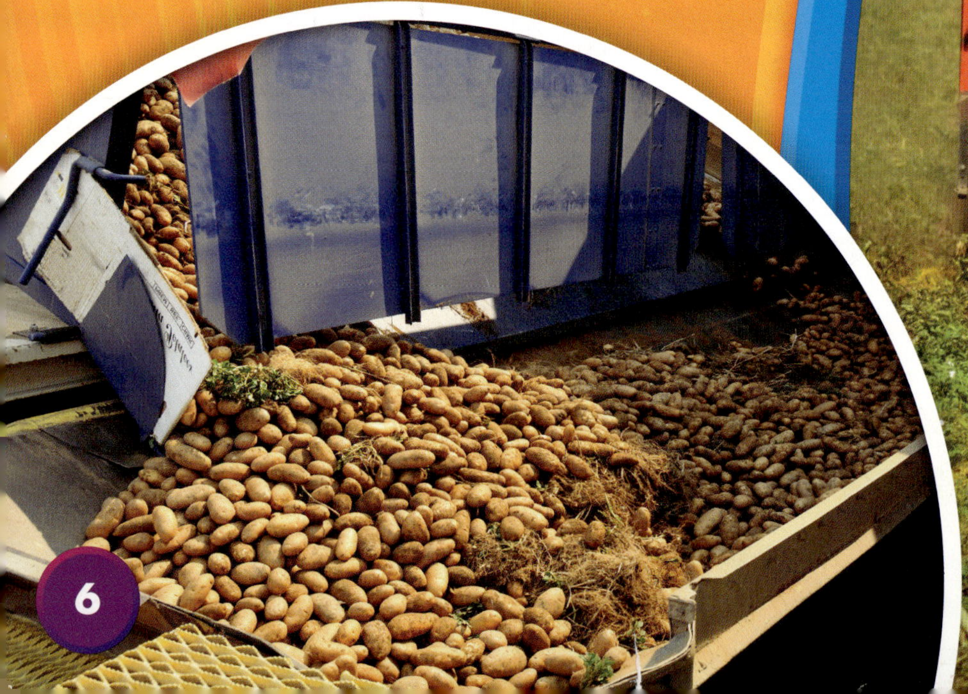

Potato Types for French Fries

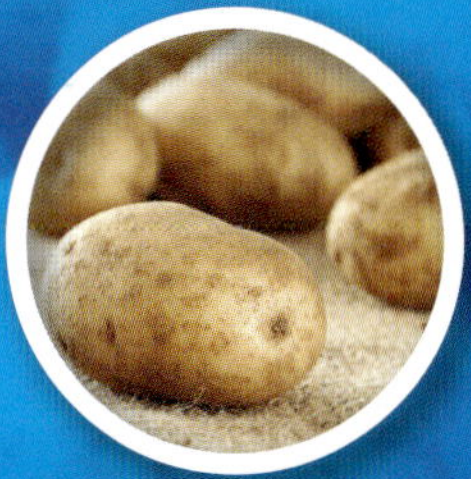

russets

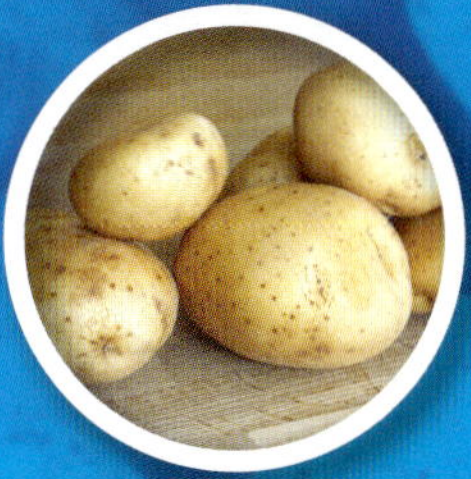

maris pipers

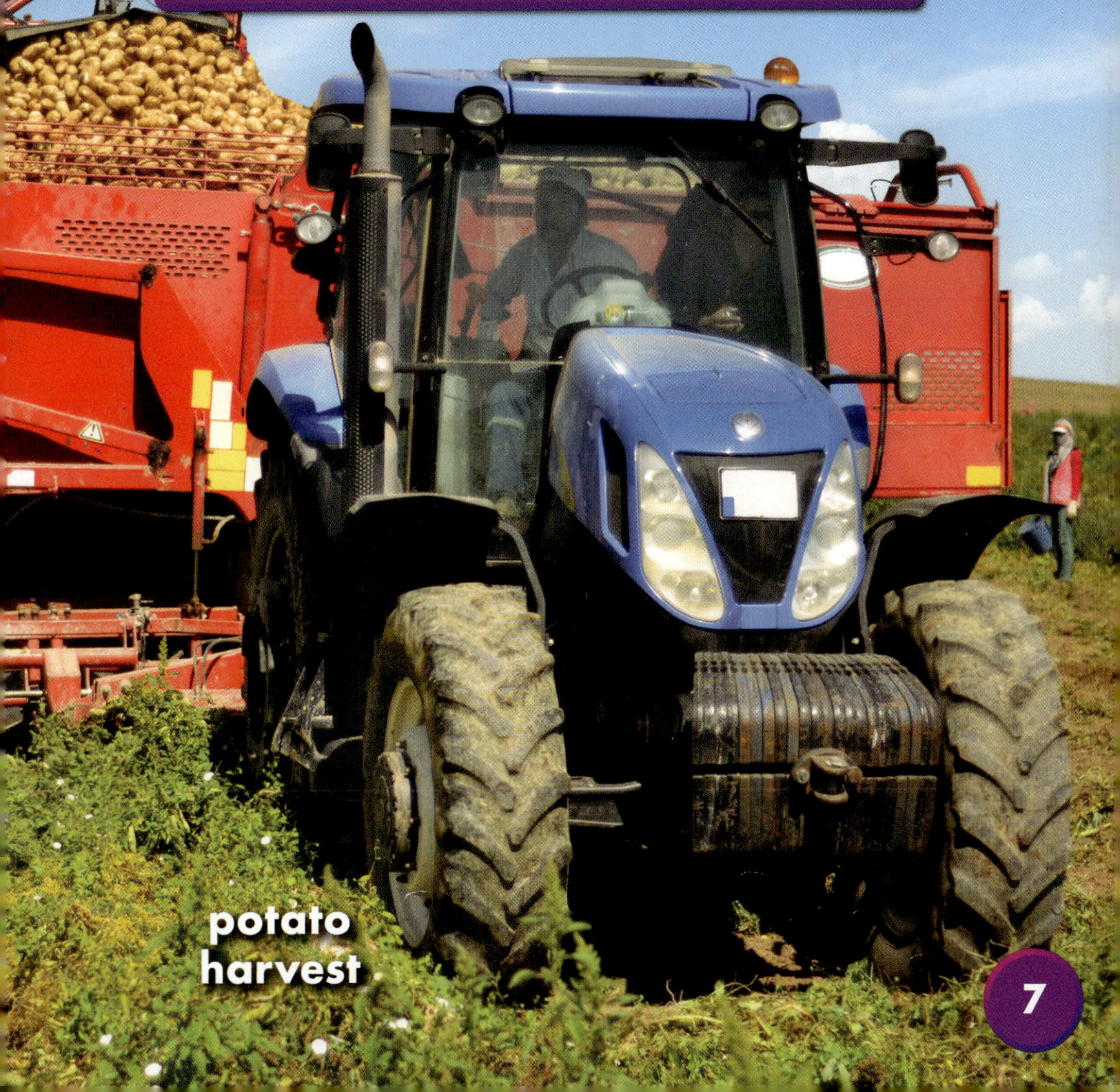

potato harvest

At the factory, the potatoes travel along **rollers**. The rollers remove dirt and **eyes**.

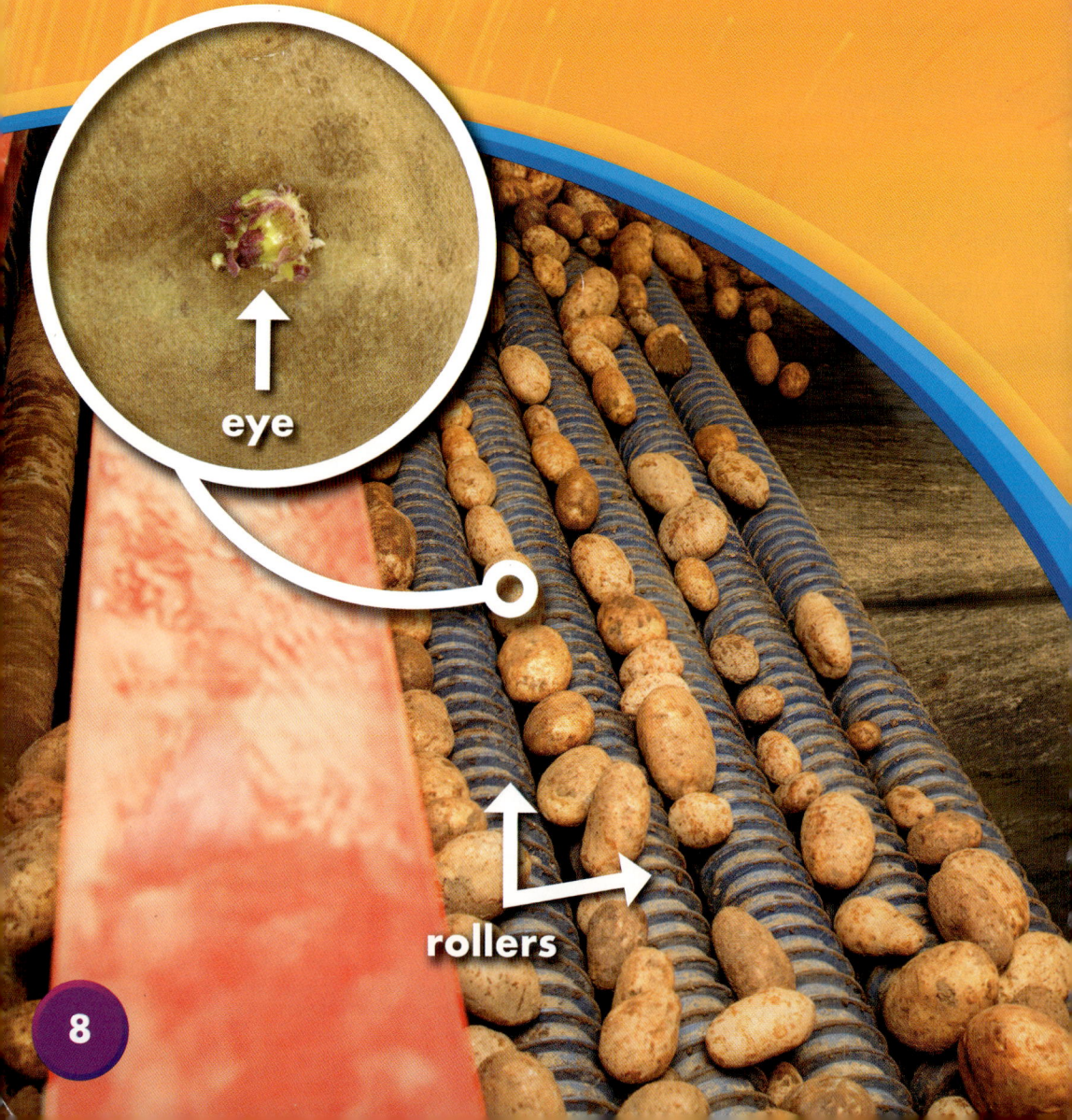

eye

rollers

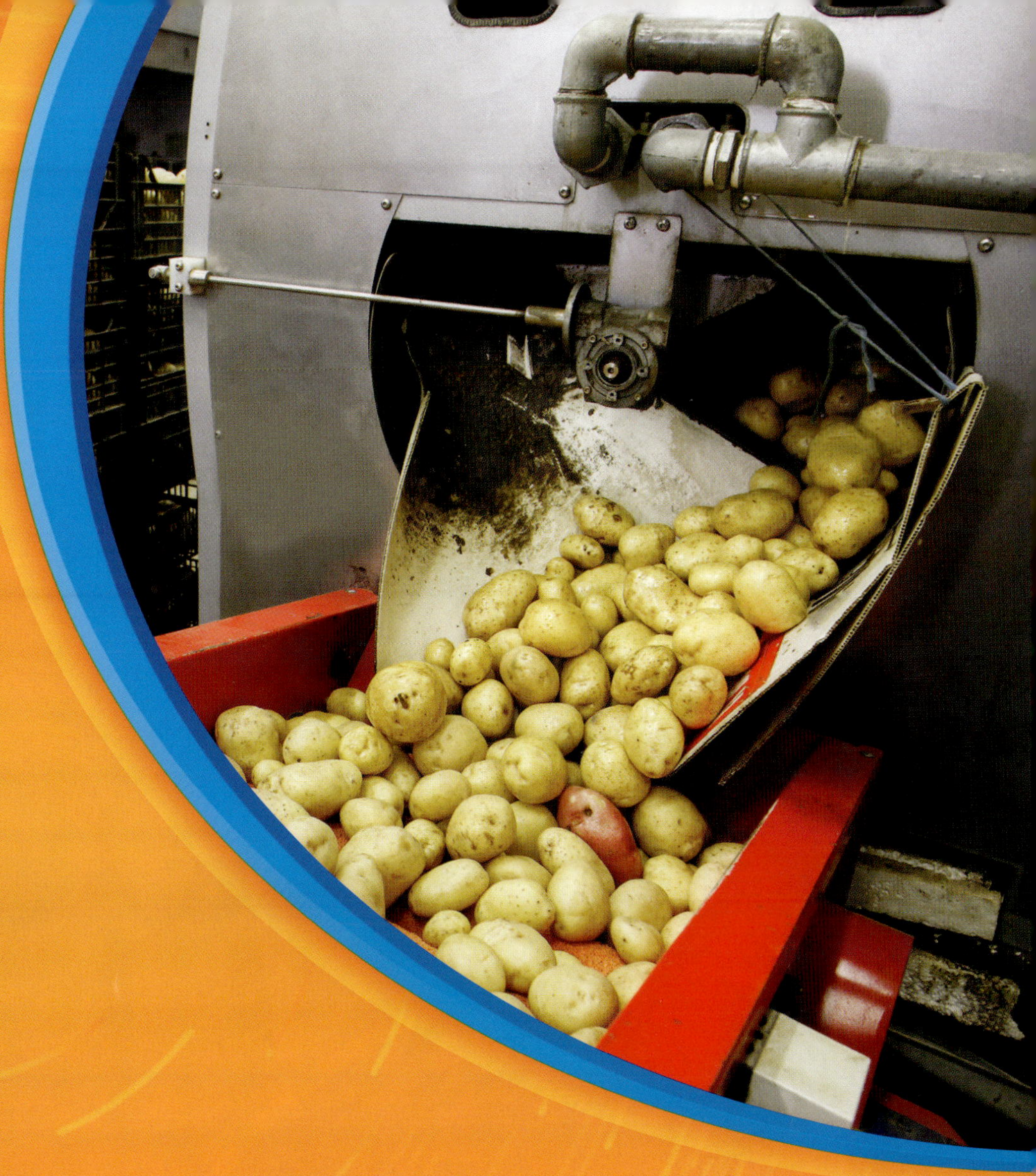

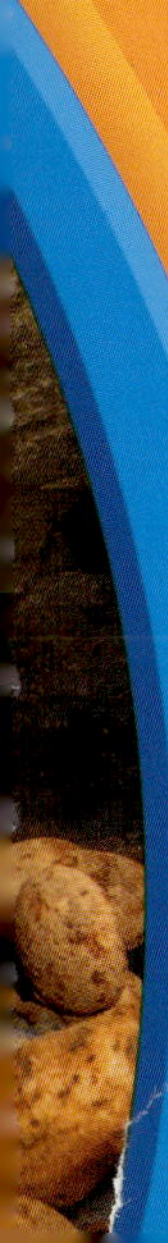

Afterwards, the potatoes are washed and sorted by size.

Next, the potatoes travel to a **steamer**. The steamer softens the potato **skins**.

The steamed potatoes travel to the **peeler**. Jets of water gently remove the skins.

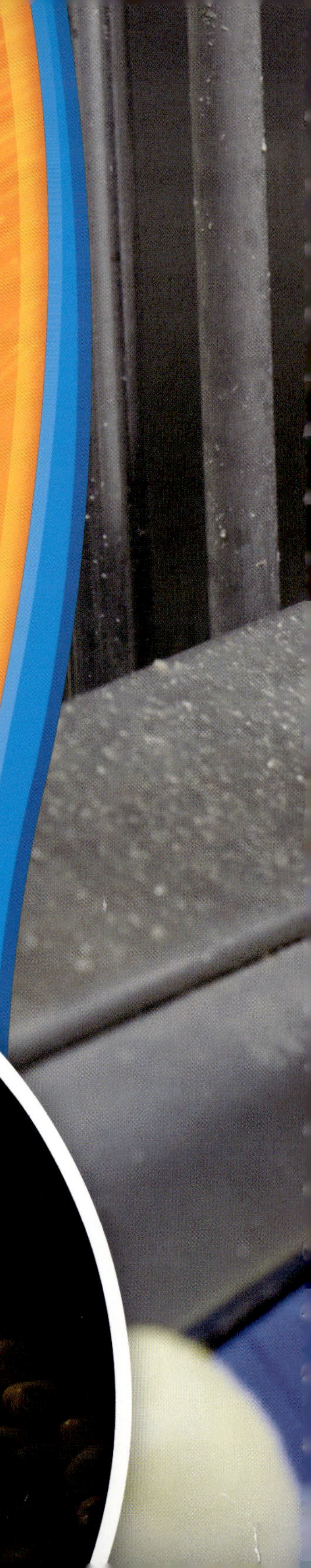

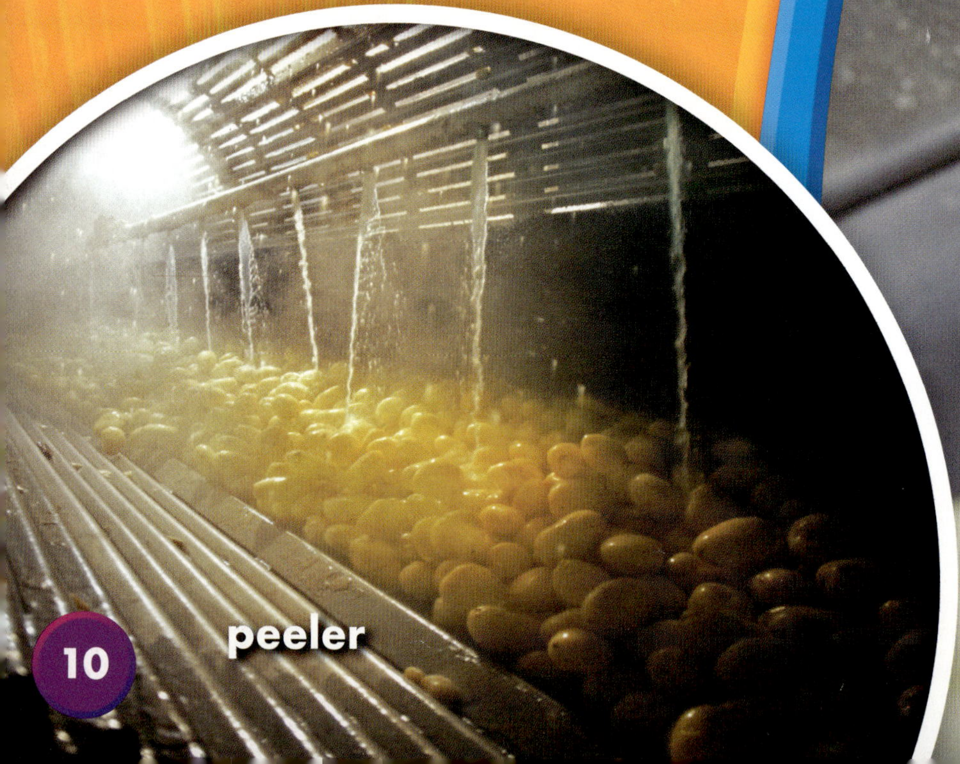

peeler

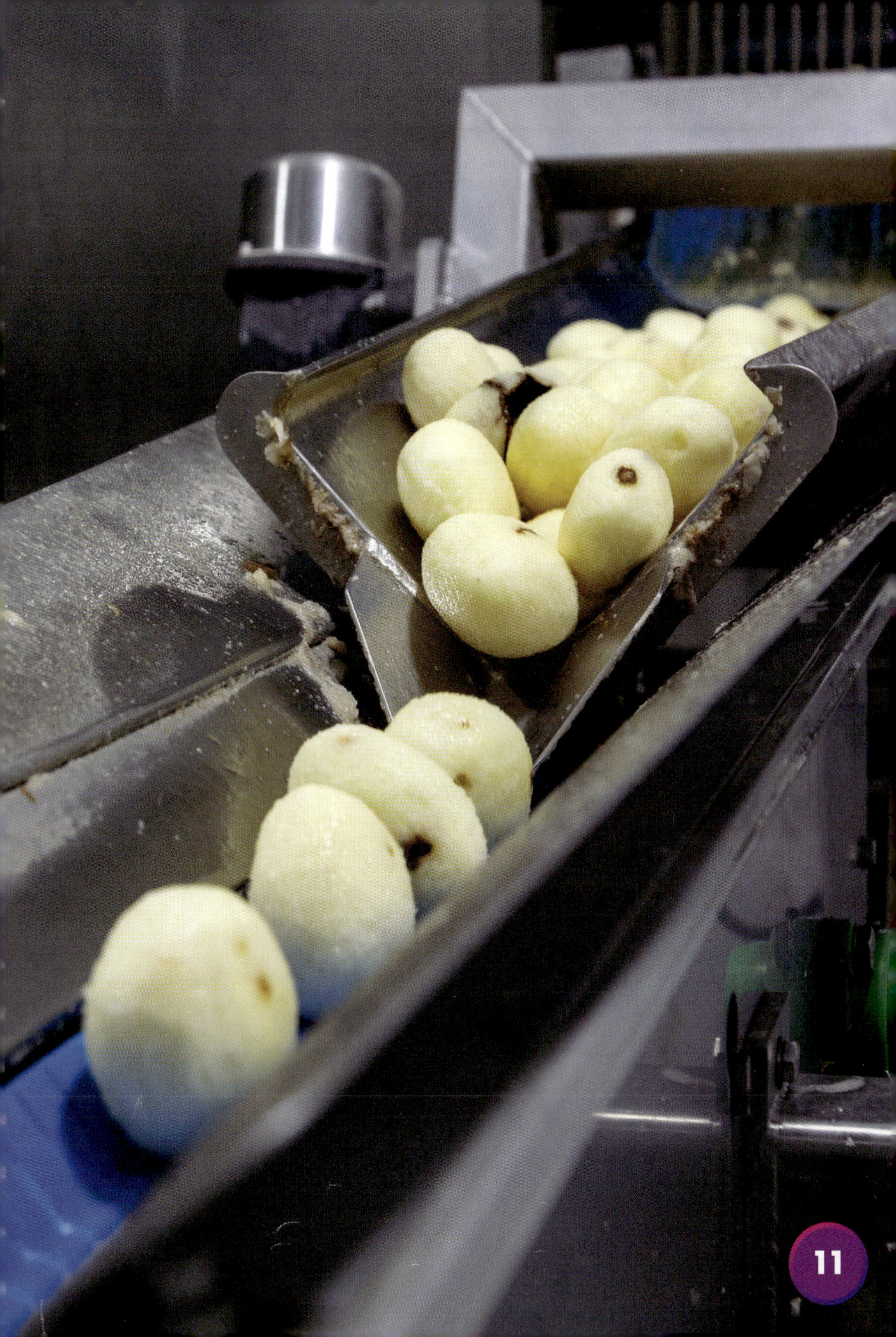

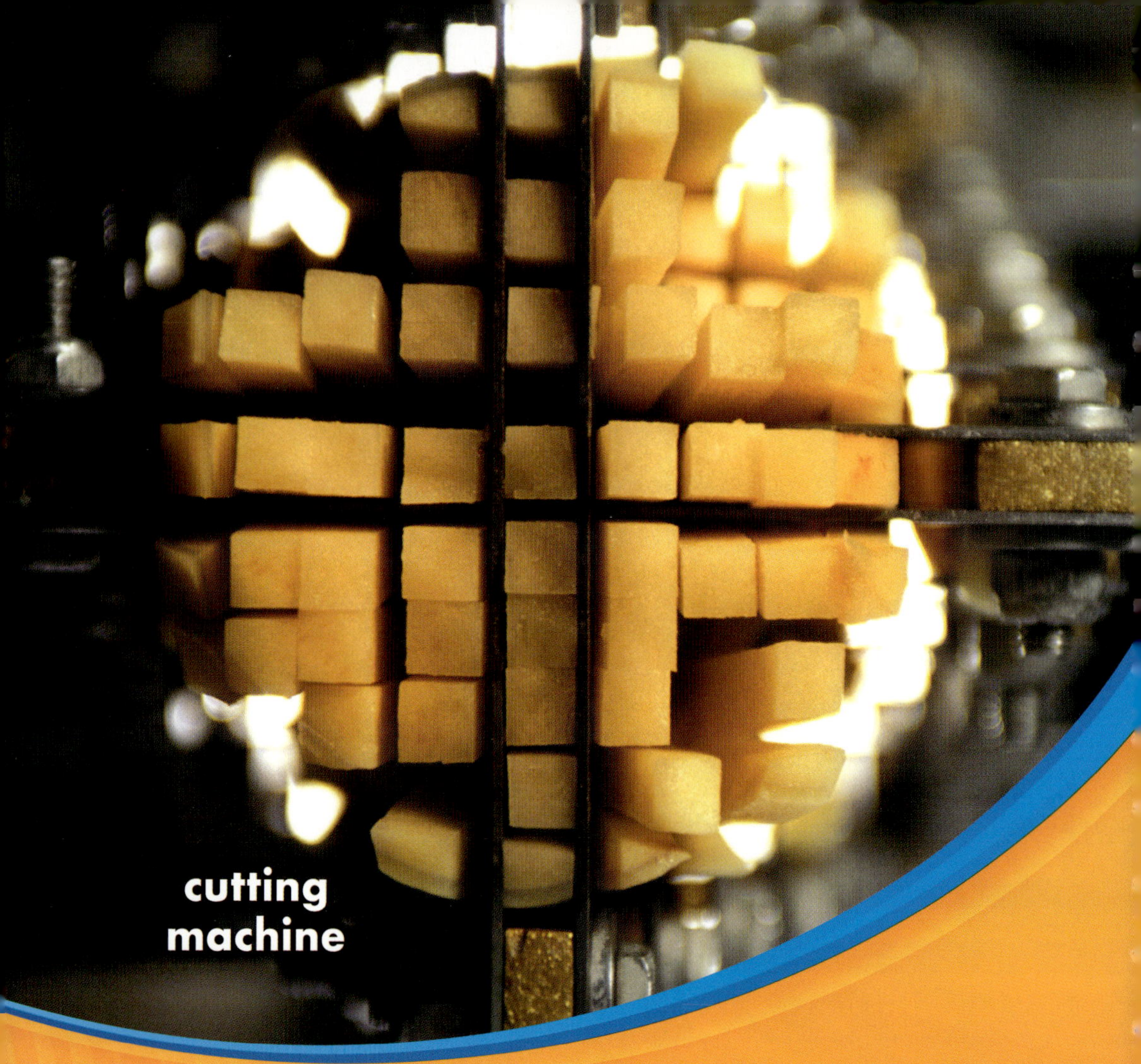
cutting machine

The potatoes are ready to be cut. They go through a cutting machine.

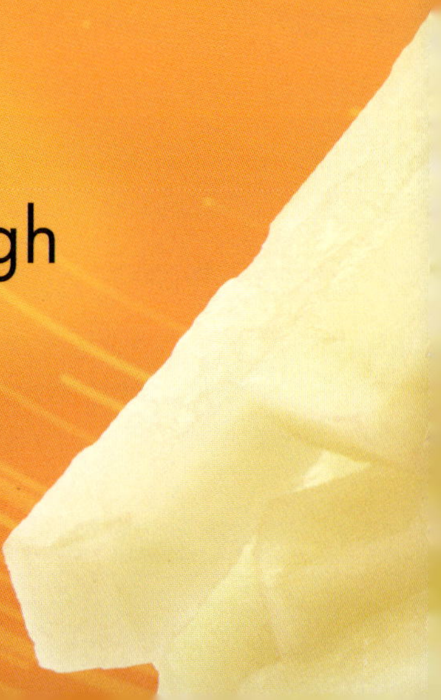

The machine cuts the potatoes into long, thin strips.

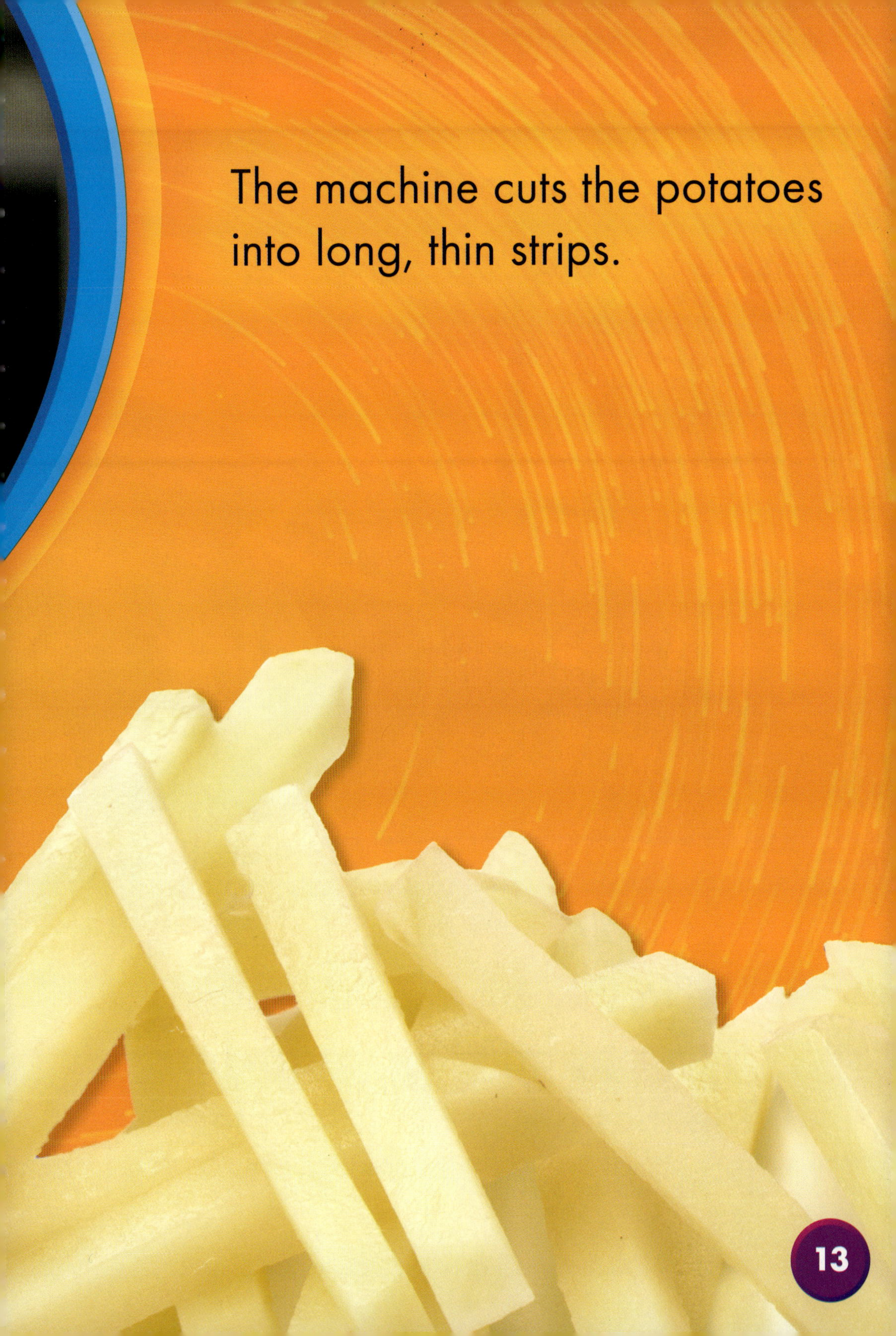

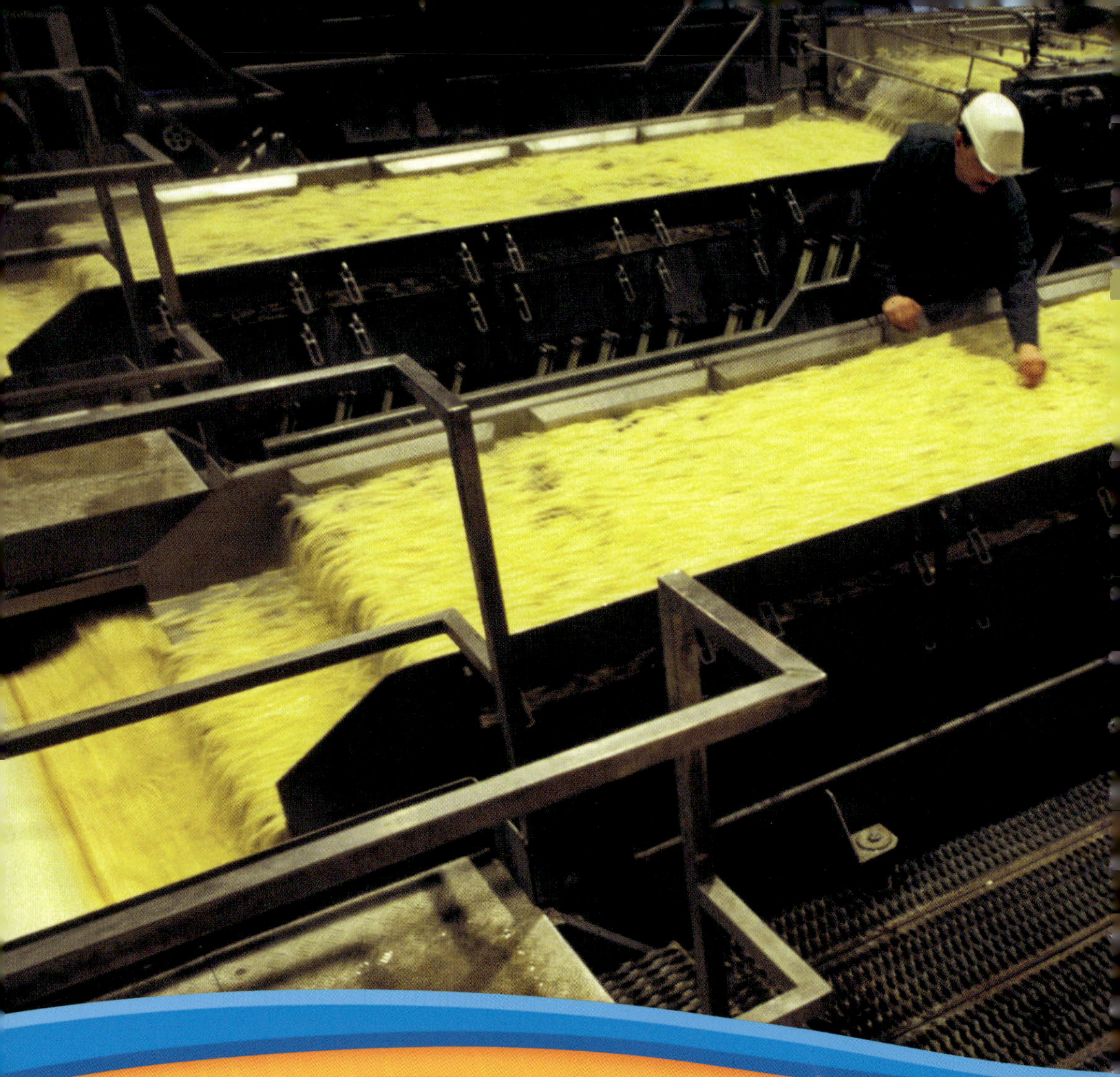

The freshly cut fries are sorted. Then they go to the **blancher**. The fries are put in hot water, then cold water.

Eating French Fries

The average American eats about 30 pounds (14 kilograms) of french fries each year!

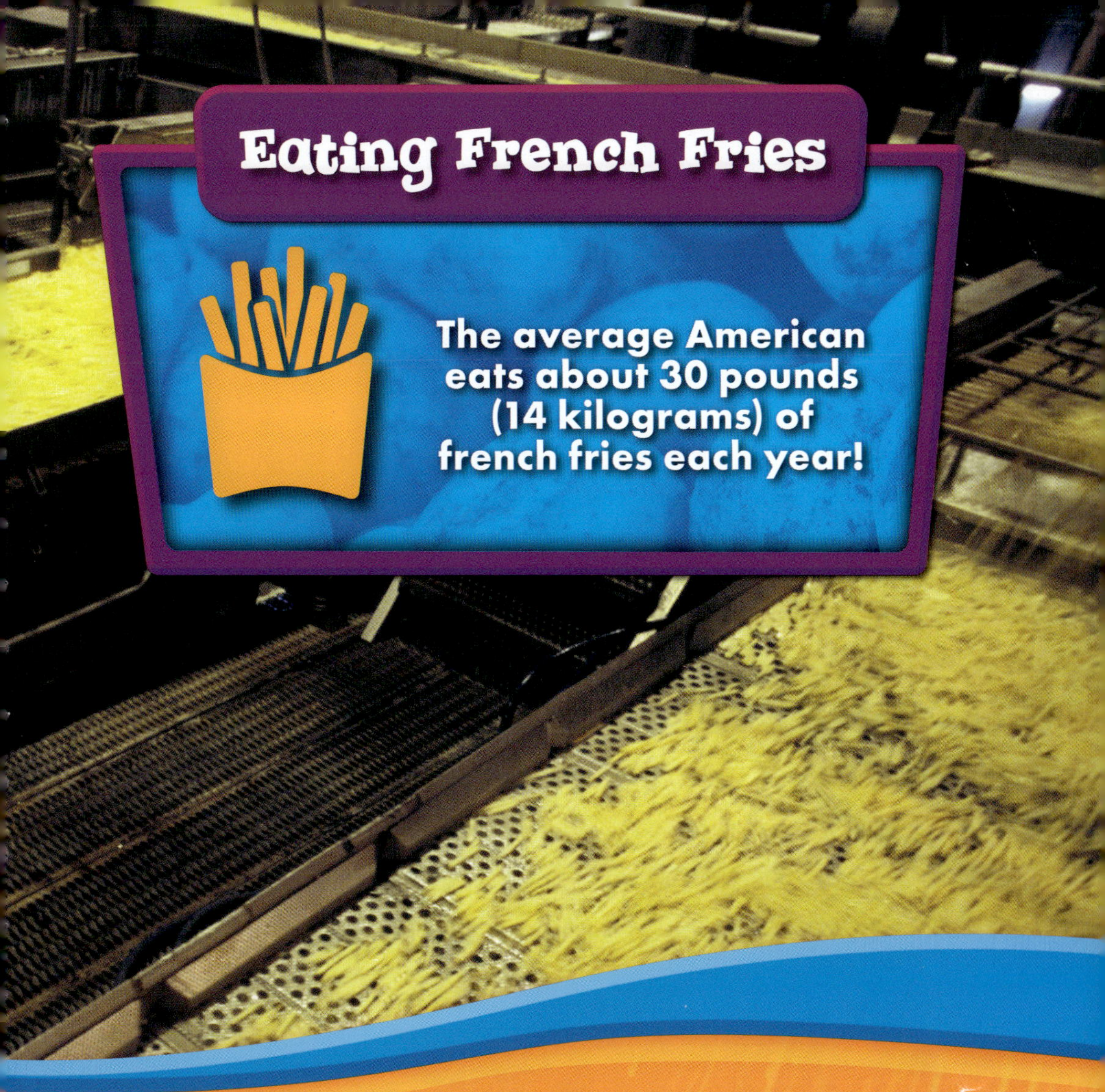

This helps them keep their **texture** and taste.

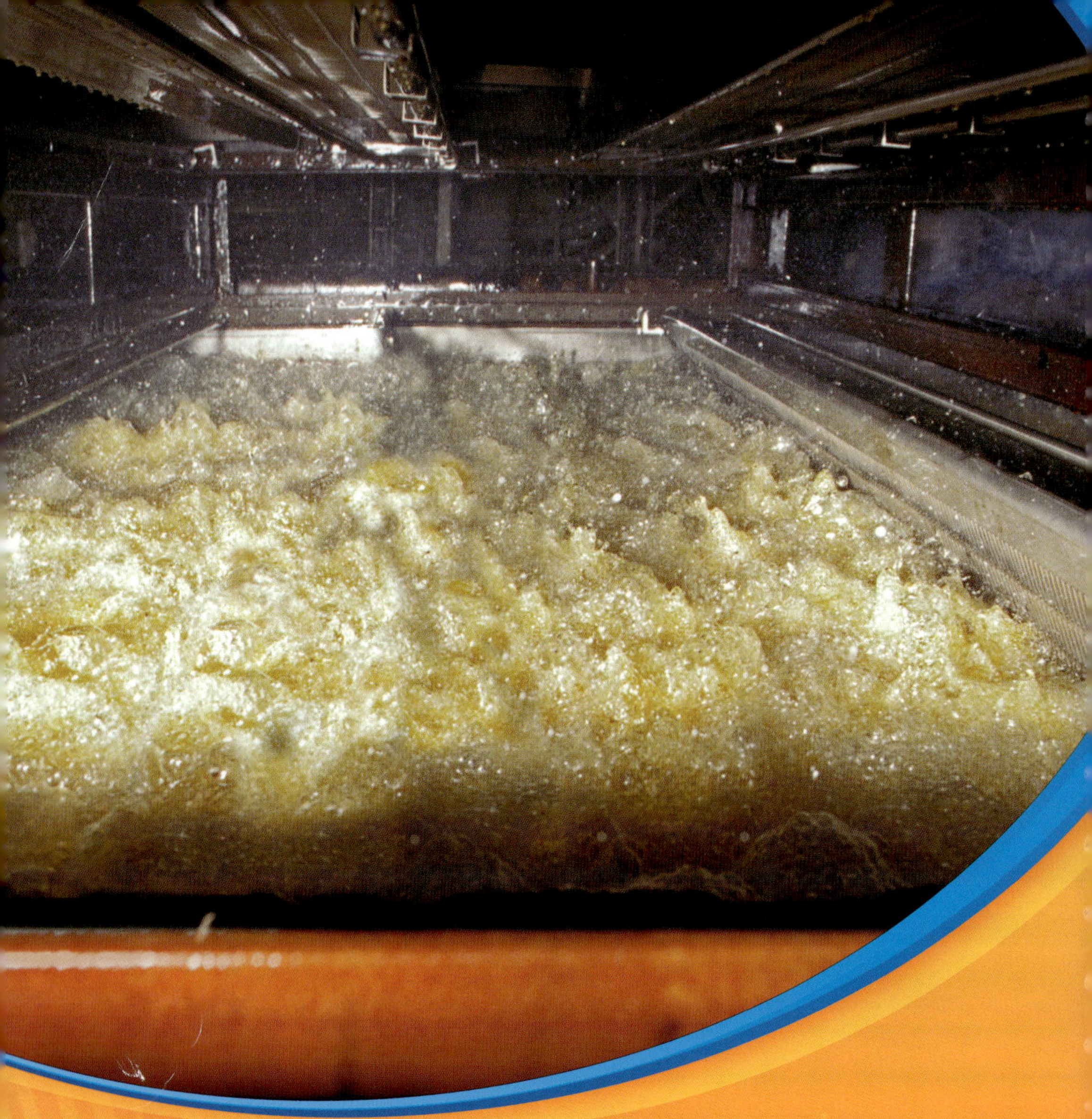

Then the fries are fried in hot oil.

Afterwards, they travel on a **conveyor belt** to the freezer.

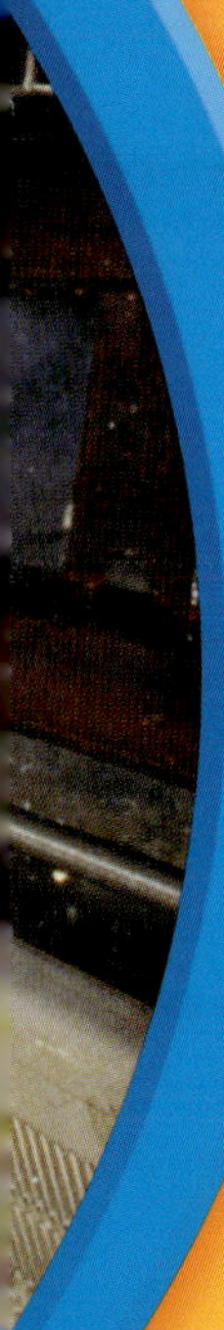

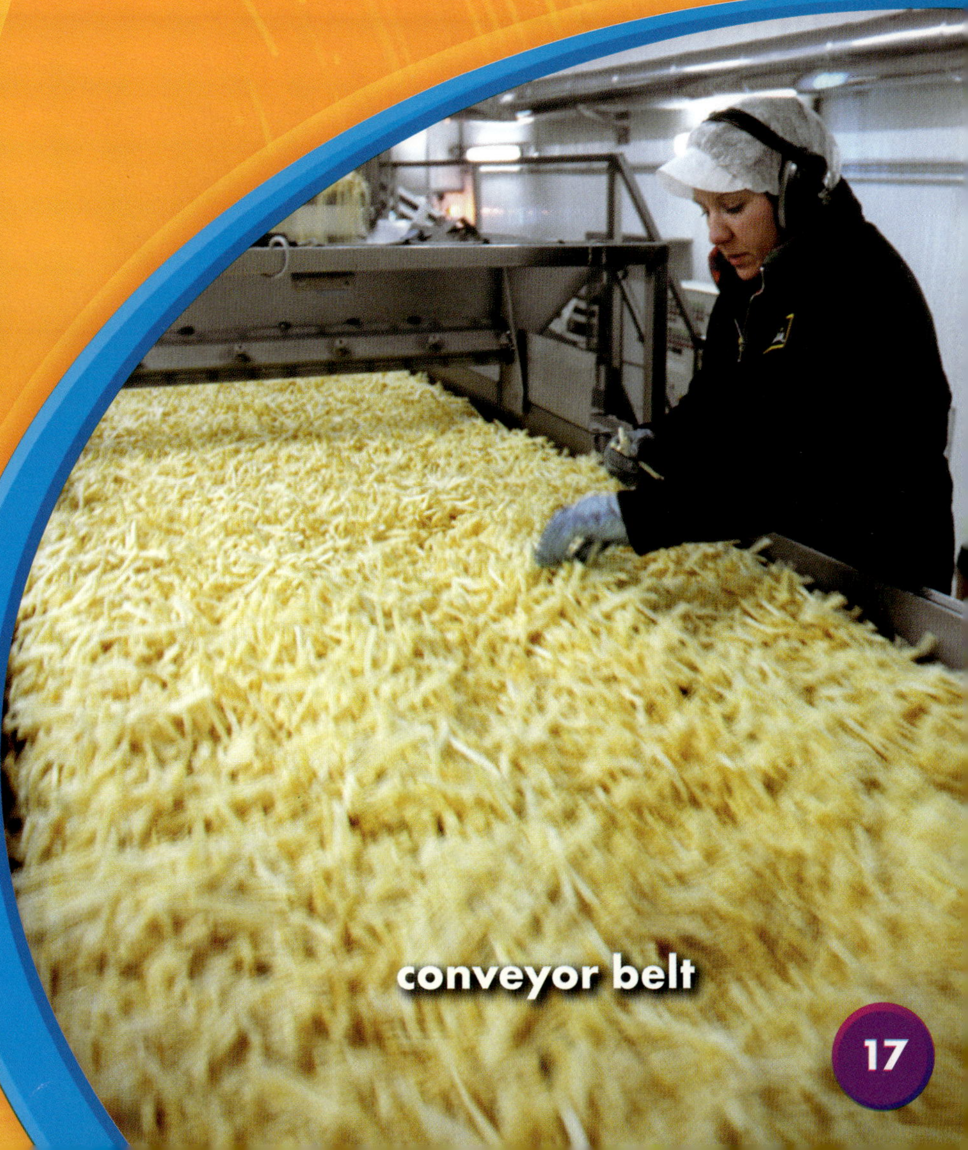

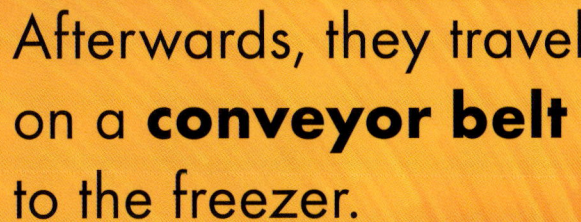

conveyor belt

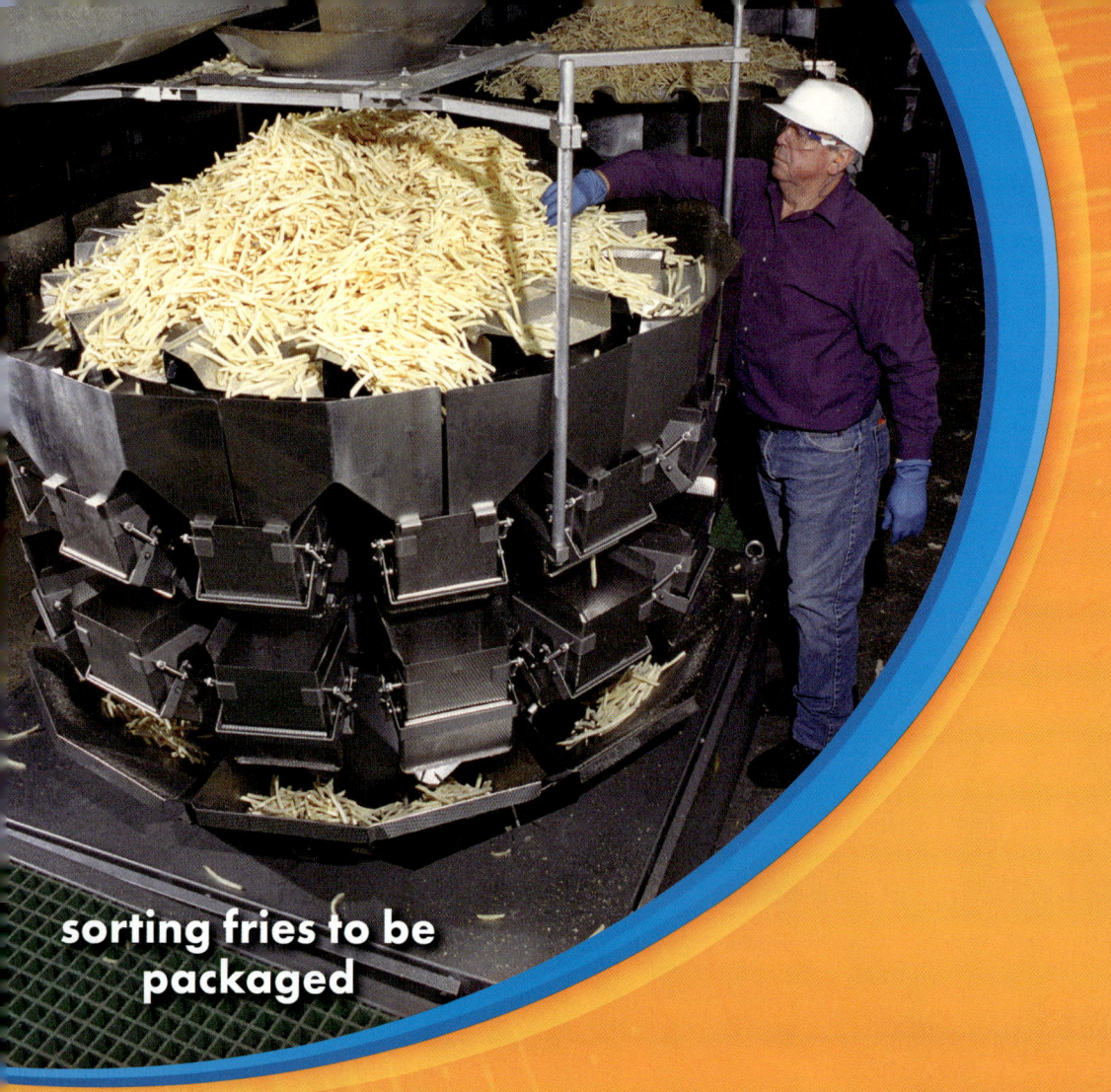

sorting fries to be packaged

Once the french fries are frozen, they are packaged into bags. The bags are sent to stores and **restaurants**. The fries are ready to be reheated and eaten!

Potato to French Fry

1. harvest and deliver potatoes to factory

2. clean and sort potatoes

3. steam and peel potatoes

4. cut and blanch fries

5. fry fries in oil

6. freeze, package, and deliver fries

A Tasty Snack!

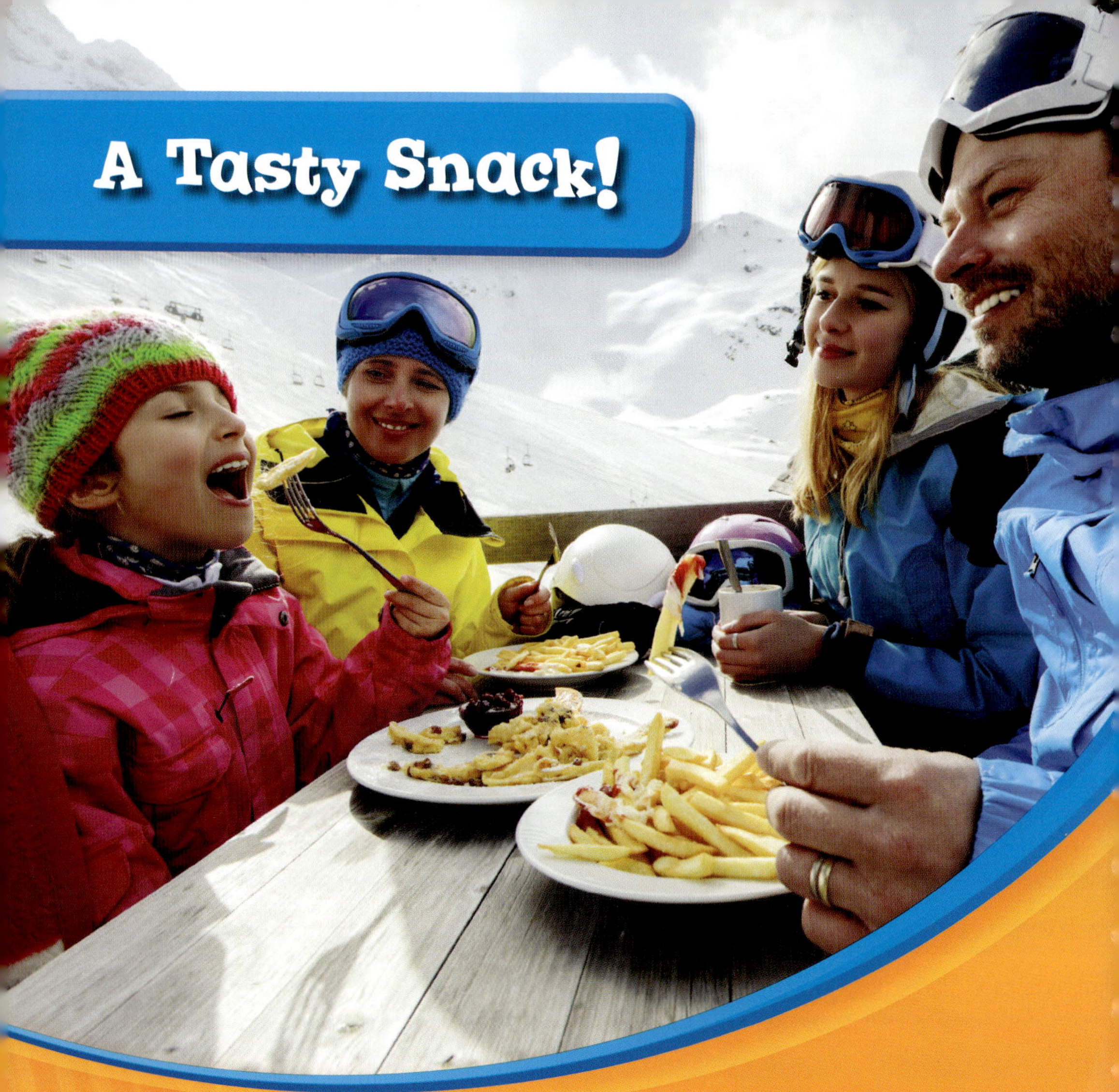

French fries come in many shapes and sizes. Some people add toppings like salt and ketchup.

There are many ways to enjoy this tasty snack!

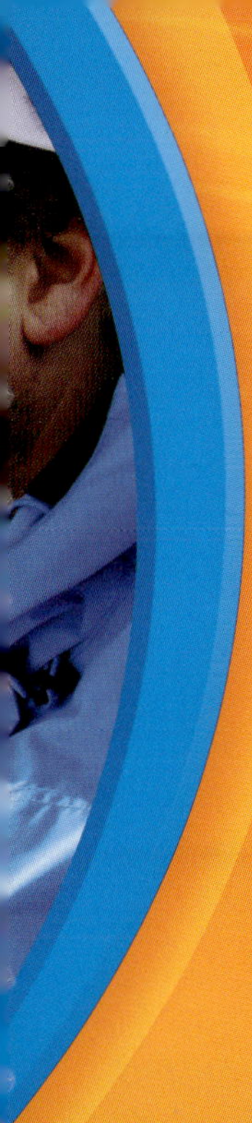

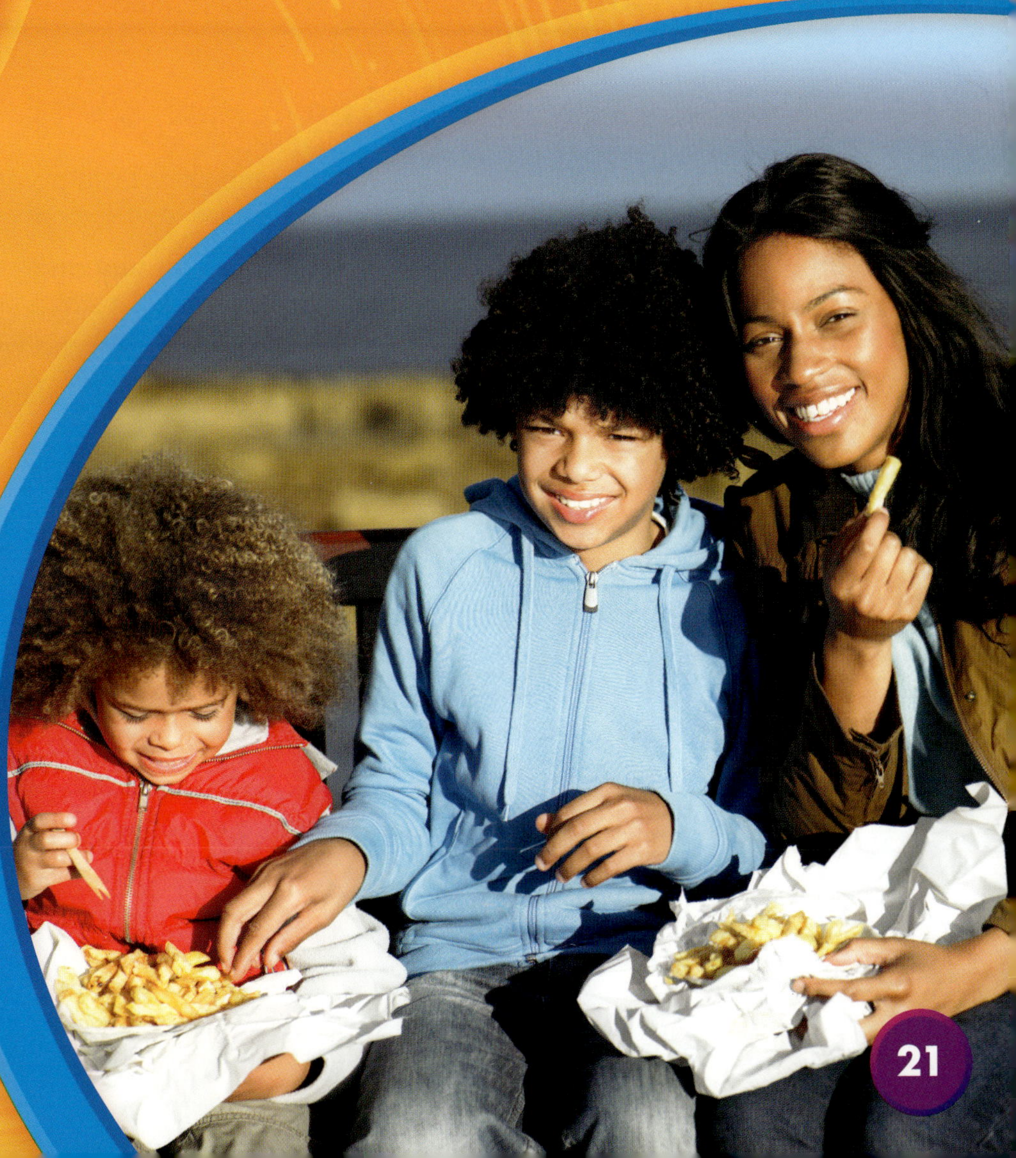

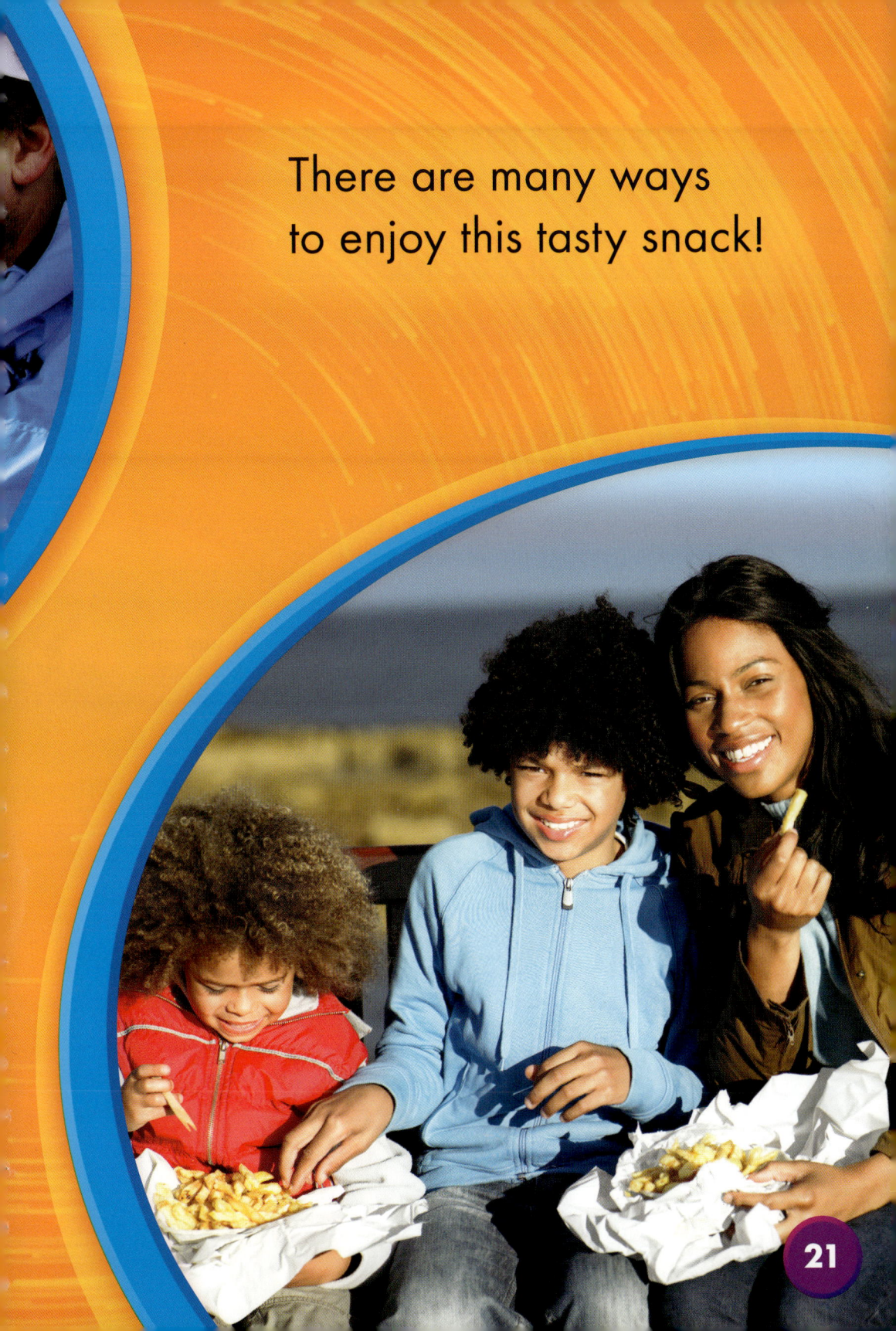

Glossary

blancher—a machine that heats and then cools potatoes so they stay fresh

conveyor belt—a device that moves things from one place to another

eyes—potato stems that are not fully formed

harvest—to gather crops

peeler—a machine that removes the skins from potatoes

restaurants—places where people can buy and eat meals

rollers—devices that remove dirt and eyes from potatoes

root vegetables—vegetables that grow under the ground

skins—the outer coverings of potatoes

steamer—a machine that uses steam to soften and loosen the skins on potatoes

texture—the feel and appearance of something

To Learn More

AT THE LIBRARY

Bell, Samantha. *Potato Harvester*. Ann Arbor, Mich.: Cherry Lake Publishing, 2017.

Mattern, Joanne. *French Fries*. Minneapolis, Minn.: Bellwether Media, 2020.

Ransom, Candice. *French Fries*. Minneapolis, Minn.: Pop!, 2019.

ON THE WEB

FACTSURFER

Factsurfer.com gives you a safe, fun way to find more information.

1. Go to www.factsurfer.com.
2. Enter "potato to french fry" into the search box and click 🔍.
3. Select your book cover to see a list of related content.

Index

bags, 18
blancher, 14
conveyor belt, 17
cutting machine, 12, 13
eating french fries, 15
eyes, 8
factories, 6, 8
farmers, 6
farms, 5
freezer, 17, 18
grow, 5
harvest, 6, 7
oil, 16
peeler, 10
potato harvesters, 6
restaurants, 18
rollers, 8
root vegetables, 5
seasons, 6
skins, 10
snack, 21
sorted, 9, 14, 18
steamer, 10

steps, 19
stores, 18
taste, 15
texture, 15
toppings, 20
types of potatoes, 7
washed, 9
water, 10, 14
where potatoes grow, 5

The images in this book are reproduced through the courtesy of: Atiwat Witthayanurut, front cover (french fries); Ttatty, front cover, (potatoes); mahirart, p. 3; Chad Hutchinson, pp. 4-5; Richard Thornton, p. 6; efhialties, pp. 6-7, 19 (step 1); Brent Hofacker, p. 7 (russets); joingate, p. 7 (maris pipers); Louella938, p. 8; georgeclerk, pp. 8-9; zilikovec, pp. 9, 19 (step 2); Patrick Landmann/ Science Source, pp. 10, 12-13, 14-15, 16, 17, 19 (steps 3, 4, 5); National Farmers Union/ Alamy, pp. 10-11; Nattika, pp. 12-13; David R. Frazier Photolibrary, Inc./ Alamy, pp. 18, 19 (step 6); gorillaimages, pp. 20-21; oliveromg, p. 22; Billion Photos, p. 23.